Winner of the 2000 Backwaters Prize

DAVID STAUDT

The Gifts and Thefts

The Backwaters Press

821
S

First Printing: 750 Copies, June, 2001

Published by The Backwaters Press,
3502 N 52nd St, Omaha NE 68104-3506.
gkosm62735@aol.com,   (402) 451-4052
www.thebackwaterspress.homestead.com

ISBN: 0-9677149-4-X

Printed in the United States of America by Morris Publishing
3212 E Hwy 30, Kearney NE 68847

Acknowledgments

Antietam Review: "Amusement," "Cold," "Franklin Heights"

Appalachian Heritage: "Hawks"

Blueline: "Billboard," "Coop," "Preacher's Camp"

Buffalo Spree: "Shining Willow Gall," "Cabbage Moths Settling for the Afternoon"

The Cape Rock: "Bless These," "White Acre"

Carolina Quarterly: "Red Sumac," "3 Stars"

Chattahoochee Review: "A Good Date," "A Reading," "Drunks Handling Lines in Seattle"

Dickinson Review: "Souls"

Endless Mountains Review: "Deep Depth," "Milt," "The Chrysler," "Staff Sergeant Woodrow Staudt," "300 Hills"

5 AM: "1968," "Warships," "Bachelor Officers Quarters, Dam Neck 1987"

Fresh Ground: A Poetry Annual: "At the Naval Nuclear Prototype, Ballston Spa"

Greensboro Review: "Night in the Box," "Rattlesnake," "Temporary"

Laurel Review: "Little Brown Bat"

Nassau Literary Review: "Lehighton"

New Zoo Poetry Review: "White Tent in the Alleghenies"

Now and Then: "Aunt Emmy, Little Jenny"

Painted Bride Quarterly: "Asthma" "Bake Oven Knob," "Northeast Extension," "Packerton," "Spike," "Running Ultra Quiet," "Tioughnioga River Bottom"

ProCreation: "The Light in Fall Creek"

River Oak Review: "Submariners," "New Pain on the River," "Finding a Map of Blue Mountain," "Incident"

Southern Humanities Review: "Dream of Pines"

Sunrust: "Sea Smoke"

Visions-International: "Rondeau"

Westminster Review: "Remembering Eustis, Florsida"

Zone 3: "Return to Port, December"

Many thanks to the supporters of The Backwaters Press, whose generous contributions and subscriptions have made possible the publication of this book.

ANGELS
Steve and Kathy Kloch
Greg and Barb Kuzma
Don and Marjorie Saiser
Rich and Eileen Zochol

BENEFACTORS
Barbara Schmitz

PATRONS
Guy and Jennie Duncan
Cheryl Kessell
Maureen Toberer
Frederick Zydek

SPONSORS
Paul and Mildred Kosmicki
Gary Leisman and Wendy Adams
Jeff and Patty Knag
Matt Mason
Pat Murray and Jeanne Schuler
Anne Potter
Carol Schmid
Alan and Kim Stoler
Don Taylor

FRIENDS
J.V. Brummels
Twyla Hansen
Tim O'Connor
Jim and Mary Pipher
Richard White

DAVID STAUDT

The Gifts and Thefts

In memory of Ruth Arnold, daughter of Mag,
Eustis, Florida, 1929,
"the outgoing one,"

and for her strong and beautiful daughters

Contents

One

One

Maybe nothing ever happens once and is finished. Maybe happen is never once but like ripples maybe on the water after the pebble sinks, the ripples moving on, spreading, the pool attached by a narrow umbilical water-cord to the next pool which the first pool feeds, has fed, did feed, let this second pool contain a different molecularity of having seen, felt, remembered, reflect in a different tone the infinite unchanging sky, it doesn't matter: that pebble's watery echo whose fall it did not even see moves across its surface too at the original ripple-space, to the old ineradicable rhythm thinking *Yes, we both Father. . . .*

—William Faulkner
Absalom Absalom

Remembering   Eustis,   Florida

It was work the hands could remember,
like rubbing the silk from shucked cobs,
or shinning the scales off 8¢ mullet,
so she picked and kneaded Kleenex
into little piles, and each visit
we brought the old woman more white tissues
and a cool tin of Railroad snuff sneaked
past the desk in our mother's clutch purse.
The snuff raised a burn in the gum,
and balanced the burning in her lower gut.

A woman that light and that long in bed
becomes less body than relief:
a woman of wood in raised relief
my sisters and I circled shyly,
ignorant of her story. Mag Arnold,
Mag, was a pixie's name, a name
for a pioneer bride, and I pictured
lean caymans bumping together like rafts
on Dora Canal, swampland magnolia pink,
a woman in silt to the knees, slogging
dripping cabbage.

Easter, mother cried
all day in her weak grip, remembering
Eustis, her starving lovely Old Florida,
its truck patch yield of okra, filled and paved.
We left for Allentown the next day,
so she fired a flashbulb till it burst,
her dimestore camera's thin strap
twisting into her wrist like a screw.

Eating at truck stops, fighting in the car,
how often did she stare at those
few pictures? a black-eyed doll's dollar
nightgown, its body of dried weeds,
the helpless wrinkle of a mouth
turned to explain: *It ain't my fault.*
She'd rub them gently in the dark,
just as we children in the back seat
sometimes silently fingered the face
of a woman whose name was *Liberty*
on our gift dollars from a century ago,
which we were strictly lectured
never to lose or sell.

1968

Wet white sails of the Niña, the Pinta,
my parents' sheets blow and lift on their lines
in a Saturday breeze cool as Clorox.
The queensize contours warp into hammocks
I'd like to lie in, lightly invisible.
Down the yard, my little dog twirls on her chain,
front paws in the air, by her red coop.

Barefoot mother carries wash from the cellar,
squats the basket down and her white ankles crack.
Wooden dolls of clothespins dance on her blouse,
click like clams in her pockets, make twelve
wooden fingers on hands that taste like bleach.
"Get off that wet rug", she says, and doesn't know
that blue bathroom rug I lie on naked
some nights listening to tubwater run
today might lift me and Smokey three feet
and carry us down to Blaine's house, could I
cry long and hard enough to make it so.

I'm crying because we can't be as poor
as the Walcks, and wear their shame for a day.
I'm crying because the carpet won't rise,
and I can't sleep on the blowing sheets,
and the little dog, who wants me, will spin
on that chain for years until she is dead.
My mom, who knows none of this, slaps wet girdles
on the clothesline, and pulls the pins apart
with her teeth, a sailor on a rolling deck,
rigging her family's bedclothes. They snap full;
slowly, the creaking earth begins to move.

Souls

In the schoolroom wing of Sts. Peter and Paul
in a Slovak district of Carbon County
an old woman teaches the lives of saints
to her second last kindergarten class.
Herself more scared of binomials and roots
than the slack-jawed stare of a Weissport hood,
at least the little ones like her, and listen
when they can, minds like whirring appliances,
opening cans of bad. This November
afternoon she feels their thin wills bend
like divining rods toward the window,
where Iron Street's oaks and weeds accept
the year's first snow. Telling the children
to put on their coats sends dust mice blowing
to the corners as she winds a nylon
babushka's daisied wrap around her head,
and marches them Indian-file,
pushing and coughing, to a fenced-in
playground no bigger than a carport.
At the bottom of Iron Street, below
the Packerton yard, the rotting roundhouse,
the Lehigh makes its last white run,
boiling in cold, before the long freeze;
the dark hills fade to pony gray.
"Look into the sky," Sister Pamela says,
"Pretend you are the top of a mountain"—
the snow ticks zooming up their nostrils,
her thick specs watering like beer glasses,

dizziness when snowflakes stop mid-air,
and the body starts falling into sky.
Then she tells the children how their souls
will feel, returning to heaven.

300 Hills

I never understood what Woodrow
and my father talked about
Sundays in the back of the truck,
their German nasal as Navajo
or the mutter horses make,
but knew it had to do with places
down the Union Hill and east
from Harrity to Gilbert,
or maybe the seeds in the stoppered jars,
the watermelons and hot tripe
our uncle huckstered weekly
to the poorest Dutch farmers.

"One Pound of Seeds to 300 Hills"
the Golden Cross Bantam
and Iochief Hybrid Sweet Corn
stowed in a chest of drawers
beneath the cold box where the meats
were kept, the kernels red
as caramels and wrapped
in a natural tissue. Whole counties
of stalks and stubble leavened
in that dresser, I was convinced,
each drawer packed and potent
as a brick of explosive.

Which is why our father took such care
to pick out a centworth of peas
for our garden, and used his palms

instead of the scoop, though nuggets
clung to the back of his hand,
and slid through his fingers bloated
from shavings and lathe oil.

Leaving the truck by the highway,
pulling away in the Chrysler,
I clutched my bag of free candy
raked from the shelves. I envied
his right to handle the seeds,
and thinking of the mountains
in the pound, made him tell
me for the hundredth time,
where was the half of Blue Mountain
the Staudts once owned.

Spike

Down behind the Moulthrop's diesel and rig,
a thin chain rattles across cinders
behind a small dog that barks all night,
facing a field of rye grown fathomless
and wild in the darkness. A ring-necked
pheasant pipes from its throat of steel,
and the beagle barks harder, biting off hunks
of air like an old man hit in the chest.
Next door it reminds a man who can't sleep
of a girl who can't stop crying,
her big sobs breaking like bubbles
released from a deep depth: or a weak boy
hunkered on his bed in the dark,
coaxing his lungs through an asthma attack.
Even short minutes of total quiet
seem to hum with the stress of other
people's lives, like a hospital
at close of visiting hours, everyone
silently herded to elevators.
And just as the asthmatic might try
to ease the heavy stone from his chest,
the man, to busy his hands and throat,
brews another pot of strong coffee.
The dog, its taut chain ringing the spike
in the center of its rubbed smooth circle,
pauses, sniffs, and listens.

Asthma

Only in the year of giant ragweed
does he remember the other childhood,
braced on the bed, in the high room,
how sliding into bed he'd start to drown,
rousing to the weary little music
raled through the pipes of his bronchi.
Five hours of shagging deep passes
in a friend's wet field couldn't reconcile
his body with the earth, its elemental malts
of grass dust dander brewed to toxin
in his blood. Every night for years
he practiced the stiff-valved woodwinds
of his chest, getting no better and begging
to quit, waiting for the ease and drowse
worked by a red medicine derived from coal.
Those hours the bed was a pitching raft
he clung to, dreaming of the disinfected air
of open ocean as the sports, future
friends and lives receded, the promised
healthy body of a man remained small,
and ever more sad and rare became
the girls he loved from the distance
of half a classroom, wondering
would she love me, would it matter.

Temporary

All summer I clutched at branches,
thinning Mohr's Trexlertown orchards,
sparing a pine-green Jerseyglo peach
each four to six inches of shoot.
While a scald of sunburn pinked my legs
I tore down bushels of nut-hard Elbertas
where fourteen or more buds studded a twig,
their lobes closed along a fresh suture,
so new and weak they could be rubbed off.
What was lost in number was made up in size
and ease of harvest, fewer to the ton.
I couldn't begrudge my college peers
their internships and page appointments
as each day I was hauled into the hills
in a lurching crush of high school kids
and men laid off from New Jersey Zinc,
but took my three dollars an hour in cash
doled untaxed from the back of stake truck
to prove to a union father I didn't
despise the labor, would take any work.
The first day the field boss walked the rows,
firing all the girls, then anyone who talked,
so that from the rut road the steady munch
of green wood ripping and fruit hitting ground
might have been rain passing over the hills,
drenching the field one tree at a time.
Next month on the second pass we'd strip
down the half-fleshed drupes to rot
in a wormy mash that scorched the earth,
and once, due to mysteries of subsidy
or blight, batted down rows clean of all fruit

with PVC pipes in a spasm of waste.
The squat trees looked forlorn, like bears,
circling forlornly for their stolen cubs.
To the fireman "Bill" I owned the half-truth
of having quit high school, left out Princeton
(*I couldn't take that school shit either*, he
muttered), gleaning an extra two weeks of work
when only myself and a dozen grim men
in zinc-blacked coveralls pruned to stumps
the last Oldmixon Free stand in the state:
though even we favorites lost in the end
to the busloads of Puerto Rican
regulars platooned in for the harvest,
known to have already the quality touch,
could palm the fruit down without bruising.
Afterward for weeks I spat white fuzz,
and sneaked bitter Quadrinal in hungry
swigs like bourbon from the old man's stash,
rocking in an asthmatic crouch on the bed.
I was eighteen, still two years from graduation,
the Navy recruiting station in Trenton,
beginning the years of lying for work,
willing to believe I belonged. But
someone would always know someone, or more;
someone would always have softer hands.

Palmerton by the Truckload

After her shift sewing coullottes at Scotty's,
I made my mother drive me up the highway—
the concrete, not asphalt, old state fourlane
walloping under her Valiant's bald tires—
turning around in Palmerton to let me see
the New Jersey Zinc Works by night. I'd waste
what was left of an instamatic roll
after scenic forests and one caught trout
to catch some colored lights bouncing in darkness
or one good shot of the drop forge,
the windowless sinter plant's late blood dusk,
and paint, weeks later, alone in my room,
I'm sure what must have seemed to me then
the noble desolation of industry.

How conduits' blue, descending tones
in mercury light between ladle cars
tapped the pent millennia from ore,
and raised two counties of poor dutch farmers
to optimistic lower middle class,
was the illustration I guess I sought
in those paintings true to color, lacking detail,
charmed awake those rare, sane nights
when the old man was bumped to the late shift,
and that tired woman charged for another day.

Now when the overpass crumbles,
they block all lanes through the rivergap,
for the dust must be slapped down with tar
before a highway crew, suited to walk
the moon, can seal it away in white barrels.

12

Sick soil, hazardous eight inches deep,
the government skins a street at a time
where company row homes, vacant and bagged,
root up like plumbing through a burndown.
Still the Ukrainian Orthodox dome,
bronzed again since the plant closed,
rings through Main's fried trees.

All high industry and aspiration
devolves to juvenilia now on nights
hicks plunder the foundries for scrap,
the coke stacks blasted, the spur tracks rolled,
the slag yards, dwindled in dump trucks south,
erupting untaxed in Maryland.
Everyone's schooled, enlisted, moved,
their tortured oils, pornographic nudes,
under ripped tablecloths in parents' homes
waiting to be put out of their misery.
The packed flats tarred below Chestnut Ridge
grow measurable to the eye again.
And everyone who's staying's growing old,
fading back into the land, with failed kidneys,
settling for religion and abuse.
Working the gap, a government trucks blows
potash, topsoil, algae, shit up on
the mountains, hoping something will grow.

Aunt Emmy, Little Jenny

They, too, must have watched us,
shyly, from a distance: small-boned
old Dutch women, their bunned hair
tightened shiny. Almost painful the love
brushed through a field of neck hairs,
their light hands touching
us as they passed—setting long tables,
cradling wet-bottomed shoofly,
Easters at uncle Milt's pond.
Aproned unmarried relatives,
Wie bisht, John? they would whisper,
calling us by other, older names
in a low German dying through three
centuries, gone now from Hawk Mountain.
In some old Indian religions,
our elders return as wild things,
and they mind our homes while we sleep,
cropping rhododendron from gardens,
nipping the tenderest rosebuds. We find
the perfect hoof prints, smaller than
our palms, punched through melting snow.
Those whitetail doe in the street
tonight, who's to say it isn't
Emmy and Jenny, pausing then
wheeling in our parking lights' glow,
mute and spooky and beautiful?
Who's to say that animals sometimes
wouldn't like to touch us, too?

Red Sumac

I find a shiloh in oak woods,
a peace place razed by riversilt,
possum paths tooling the high grass.
Here racks of cool white trunks lift
pecks of winterfruit, woolly staghorns.
Beyond any rise where a weed slope
dives to the first dense cloud of woods,
the pale trees halftwist northward,
tuned to the light from Polaris,
or the red star in the Little Dipper,
budding arctic nights to the stuttered
oo of the tiny, saw-whet owl.
What God sends down in lightning-hits
the earth sends back in teased wood
like a shock of frozen response,
love that goes only out, pure ache.
Drawn to its damaged blooms, the holes
in hickories, the deer come out.

Bake Oven Knob

The car safe under the powerlines,
brake set, in gear, locked, forget
the back tires slipping in jolts
on chalk and grade to get here: unused
place where Lehigh Furnace Gap Road
crests Blue Mountain. A signboard stove
in sumac marks the trailhead, tells
small secrets: there is water .7
miles back, chinks in the forest
are tunnels that bore the breadth
of the eastern states. A mile up ridge,
state game road crumbles to white-blazed birch
and knife-edge, the ruin of broken limestone
damp where the mountain's spine breaks earth,
the only footing that won't grow over
two days after rain. The humid wrack
of laurel breaks at knobs and powerline cuts,
fire roads so steep and pocked a warden's
Jeep would tip. There, height is revealed
as heat, mountain curved like a dog's back,
woods peaking and rolling eight hundred feet
to brickyards of millet near Germans
and Germans Corners. Eight generations
of farmers couldn't till the rock and slope
for two hundred miles of ridge from
Delaware Water Gap west to Little
Schuykill, but hewed and scored the valleys.
Now their descendants must double back,
accepting thirst and deer ticks, blacksnakes

sumac and flies to discover
the Delaware nation of Tunkhannock,
"Endless Mountain": to feed their spirits
lean on altitude and simple fear.

Northeast   Extension

A bicyclist dives like a flea
into a pelt down a road you just
glimpse from an overpass, but here,
at the land's right level, where
the turnpike fits by trestle and
berm the lapped and puckered woods
of eastern townships—the Quakers'
Great Swamp, the Delaware Shades
of Death—a favoring sea of leaves
rolls under the highway to ridges
and beyond, whole counties that ripple
white before rain or bruise beneath
the weight of a cloud. Caught in the
trough between Blue and Broad or Broad
and Nescopeck Mountains, you feel
as if these rollers had traveled
days from the center of a great
monsoon, promising steeper grades
and gale of traffic, banks of inland
cities north, interstates whipping
like the deadliest wind for hundreds
of miles from an eye you imagine
windless: as if all geography turned
around a hillside south of Vestal,
where the feedcorn sags through a post
rail fence, the rails have not moved
for fifty years, and a puzzled
hawk drifts to a stop in the sky,
without a draft to tend her either way.

Billboard

By day a wooden wall above the barb-
wired prison courtyard of the turnpike:
the first barn's last surviving side,
its back boards bearded by a cowbird's nest,
imbued with a creosote of leaded smoke.
A celery salt of rust and powdered moth
parts glitters in the cattails, their woolly
pones risen to butt a painter's plank,
where a gypsy moth's unpopped kernel
sticks to a lantern. Three hours before
the sun goes down the lights snap on,
triggered by the smallest shift to red
in amber weeds along a drainage ditch,
or possibly one cricket's lower creak
that dragged the field's hum half a herz.
Later the farmer's wife will see them
wading down into the fields: combines
harvesting bales of white mosquitoes,
driven down the pike from Philly or
Scranton like reapers from the regions
of light, taking, for now, only
what's cheap and most common.

Hawks

Hunters loved to shoot into the clouds
and fell a shock of feathers
into woods below Bake Oven Knob,
slopes too steep to send a dog down.

They migrate here again, red-tailed
and sharp-shinned hawks, recover
the state by rivergap and overpass,
crop moles from turned fields

or lift loose poults
behind corncribs. Sniping crows
can't hinge a goshawk's
locked wings as it drags

the shallow of treetop nests.
So many trace the highways now
you could believe the land
had split its wilder seams,

mugwort and chickory crack
our roads, creeks dry up in garlic
and even cornstalks' rebel cobs
sprout purple kernels.

Roadside   Crosses

White and cleanly carpentered
as Baptist churches they surprise
us at the riverbank shoulder
of a merge lane, trailing a bunting
of ribbon and silk hibiscus
while a factory restlessly
broods through its night shift
across a cinder parking lot.
Or stand self-conscious but inscrutable
by roads laid straight through soft
fields buffered with hillocks of
softer sawgrass: Lisa, 9; Lois,
40; Cheyenne, 3; petitioners
in ironed workweek clothes they rise
through natural bashfulness ignorant
of the legalities of tragedy
to make a citizen's plain statement.
All across the country these rivets
tack the upholstery of our
memories and care to the land,
lest we drift too high into the
country of plans and anxiety,
bicker and regret, climbing at
seventy miles per hour with reckless
inattention to each other.

Tioughnioga River Bottom

Dry summers in the central counties,
Cayuga, Tioga, Cortland, New York,
the broad creeks drain down clear,
and rivers thin to licks and kills
painted over sheetrock bottoms.
Crows follow gulls onto dry bed
recently abandoned by alewives,
wary of new ground barren and white
as the moon's. On Fall Creek herons
lift their oars and pull hard overhead
for deeper water. In hipboots
you can walk some rivers for miles,
ascending steps and slabs of shale
flagged as cleanly as roman roads
paving the remotest provinces,
now sunken and graffitied with
the pebble spits of crawfish.
The relic gates and vaults revealed
in sunlight through water cider dark
that is the last issue of glaciers
we know were sealed when the world
was younger and latent, though even
now strange mouths dimple the river.
Often in these late dry days of
disclosure, the scattered infidel
children of Vandals and Palatines
forage these ruins, trying to charm
with a caddis of elk hair jewels
of prehistory all muscle and light.

The Light in Fall Creek

A deer in the gorge, in fog,
is taking her fawn across Fall Creek.

The river's muddy and high after storm,
the fawn's belly sops dark water.

He's white-spotted sorrel, the mother buff.
She turns him like a sailboat

in tack, holding the small deer to leeward,
close, probing a hoofhold of shallow.

Down the bank, you have to ford the trail sideways:
bush sunflowers, ostrich-ferns, neck-high

and wet. You must feel your way
with your feet; there are muskrat holes

in the path; it would help to have
a clearing or blaze to shoot for.

Pulsing through drizzle on the creek's far bank
like purple magnesium sparklers,

something has touched off the teasel.

Little Brown Bat

It comes in with a belly full
of beetles when the rain begins,
making for gable or steeple
up walls its ultrasonic chirp
illuminates like heat lightning.
Finds the chewed hole, the cubby, peace.
In the chapel one little
Myotis has crawled on its stump
of folded wing and barbed ankle
to the middle of a crossbeam,
and sits in clean light from below,
battered pugface basking in a cloud
of scent and soured aftershave.
Biased for mosquito-whine or
hawk-moth hum, its lightly furred
attentive ears can't hear the slow
hymn moaned in the pews, only
the delightful screams: the highest
harmonics of piano wires
struck under high tension. Above
the service's public expressions
of joy in guarded private pain,
only sneeze and rale of bronchi, dry
bills scraping in the acolyte's plate,
the tick of spent nerves firing
in soliloquy. How wonderful
the sonic bath high in the warm
rafters! The chords struck *in extremis!*
The tragus within each soft ear
thrums like the pistil of a lily.

While the pianist silently
pumps the keys, and the congregation
welters in humidity, this
small composite of raptor and dog
Mohammedans claim was made by
Christ himself to tell the length
of daylight in the wilderness
(those others think was jealous work
of Satan in rare sands and clay
scoured from the ends of the earth—
lucifugus, a bungled man,
imperfectly divine), lifts its
tiny head, the moistened lips
of which seem almost human in
shape and smoothness, and smiles
with a cretin's soundless chuckle.
Animal omitted at Creation,
you might grin if you've heard your
whole life, slashing down and burning
through the atmosphere, the random
debris of the universe fizzing
like rain through a rotten roof.

Shining Willow Gall

I like to think shining willows
tell me any margin's good enough
to live on: the dry creek
seeping through the business park,
briars arrowwood alders there
oases where hidden jay chicks shriek
and leaves voles squirt through
like spit tobacco plugs. Hack
a shining willow down, the stump
will creep horizontally for years,
putting up skinny yellow shoots
in fours to the fourth or fifth power.
Sting a shining willow withe,
furry scales will overlap the hurt
to make a soft cone like a pine's,
big as a magnolia's bud.
The gall will persist all winter,
and open in March, not with petals,
but many newly lacquered wasps,
shiny and sharp as new needles.

Dream of Pines

A deer came up from the creek,
ducking the basswood and sumac.
Over the course, it began to snow.
The golfers played through.

It could see, like I could, the rare
late velvet of the fairway
lifting the way a pond does
the morning before it freezes.

He was just a button buck
and he made me think
of the one night ray above the airport
licking low clouds like a mussel's foot,

wading toward darkness in a bank
to meet in the dry woods there
strong and beautiful sisters,
wet sides steaming in the dark.

29

Finding the Map of Blue Mountain

Like finding a fossil bird
so intact in its shell of shale
you could read the folded bones.
Or an oak sawed cleanly through,
the stump's white pith
weaving outward in threads
to mushroom heads of inky bark.
Each ring was twenty feet
and a thousand years of lifted rock,
effort both epic and silent.
A county road weeviled through the core,
the face was skived by township lines
of Heidelberg and Franklin and
the capillary of dotted line
nourishing the marrow of the ridge
was the trail for which you'd looked
for years. Now everything was named:
the few barns tenoned to crossroads,
sheds below the zinc plant,
older places west on 895,
hex and tobacco barn land,
the mite hole on the map maybe
the house where your father was born.
You treasured it greater than
Bible or poems, that perfect
translation of everything seen
as a kid from a car's backseat

into its adult word, its only
motive clarity. And wandered
in its whorls of dense topography
long after you left the region
for good, stopped reading or believing.

Rattlesnake

Just like stepping on a rattlesnake,
when you see, in quick succession,
the shadow of a branch, a branch, blacksnake,

rattlesnake, tail like a dried chili
hissing spastically, and afterward you think
I could have died paralyzed in the woods

if he'd struck, if I'd panicked, so the life
you could have led would have crushed you
had you not seen the mistake, backed out.

Just outside his striking circle you watch
him test the air in two pinholes in his face,
then stretch across the trail, each diamond

flexed deliberately, heedless of you.
Today you learn the sound of dry laurel
ticking beneath the rattler's stiff length:

you hear it all day, hiking down the mountain.
Which is not to say you've learned what sent
you here, five miles from the nearest road.

Questions About the Dry Run

Has anyone ever followed the dry run
down Star Stanton, through the maple snag?
Can one follow a dry creek bed to its end?
Do runs end cool in river, peter

to poison oak and flies, culverts in ditches
along state routes; do they ease, gravely,
to cow ponds, come out to open mountainside
at the back of a plowed field graying in heat?

What century the farmer there,
hard-faced children pulling the slope,
coming to ask your intentions?
What begins as a little water

worrying a path, high in breezy maples,
jumps its trail for the underbrush
with a broken zipper of shalestones,
a gash in topsoil diving the slope,

a swallow's flight in stone and roots
whole trees heel over at impassable tilts.
At places where it flattens to a jeep trail,
is it secretly continuing, carving air,

channeling swifts at evening,
or bushwacking up through the possible,
severing the fine-haired roots of thought?
What tall hopes fells a dry run?

I think of it up there at night, in the heat,
dry stones testing and aching, crawling
the mountain like thunder or scent,
the ardent shape of water when there's water.

White Tent in the Alleghenies

In these woods, deer shine white.
One circles circumspectly
the white handkerchief
hanging out of my pocket.
It's a forest high and empty
as a Metrodome, in which
a Minneapolis of crickets
cheers on the players all night.
At night, across the soft-leaved
floor, porcupines move in as
quietly as sailboats. One tests
the metal guard around the lean-to;
one sniffs outside my tent flap,
carefully, like someone enjoying
a steak, or trying to identify
a bad smell in the bedroom. Later,
in the car, running the heater,
listening to a Potter County preacher
pronounce evil on the government,
I hear something gnawing
on the chassis. A big one, oil-blue
and streaked ash-white, it lowers
its head in the headlight beam,
guiltily, and will not move,
like a dog caught lying on the sofa.
We sit on the ground at midnight
together, mumbling our stray thoughts.
Still later, the rest of a sleepless
night, angry red squirrels trampoline

off the tent sides. I see their rigid
bodies, airborne in moonlight, coming
toward and bouncing out of focus.
What do all the animals always
want into so much? They seem like
the poorest of the poor, dragging
their tribes across ruined plains,
and stumbling always into trouble,
as curious of their dispossessors
as shamed by their dispossession.

3 Stars

Like a different day, in which this one
muddles on, having bad dreams: above us,
in August, the winter constellations,
slow hulls crumbling aground.

Some morning see the astral dice
high between parting continents of storm,
one thousand five hundred light years in blue:
Alnitak, Alnilam,Mintaka.

How stray dogs under a street lamp,
heads up, watching you jog toward them,
leap off on suddenly slender legs,
flicking white tails.

A rare voice crisp as fox bark
calls from their gray flanks steaming in teasel.
There is another world, and it is this one,
seen through cloud or thistle.

Cold

Touching her, he wonders how she
can bear the heat of her own breasts.
It is not natural, it would seem
the body could not maintain itself,
would burn away, her arms get thin,
her shoulders dwindle to pool pockets.
He wonders how she can lie under sheets,
wrapped like an Arab while the sand
bakes from within. On a cold day she
could make a cloud. Perhaps she cannot stand
her clothes, and this is why she comes to him.
He uncoils around her like nickel
brought to the tip of a soldering rod.

Away from her he becomes solid
once again: his ribs rewind around
his lungs, banding tighter and tighter.
He thinks he must feel to her like wood,
or an old stone statute with a crack
inching the length of its thigh.
Out of his clothes he feels
like a bag stuffed with more clothes.

Lying with her at night he wants
to apologize; he feels like plastic,
keeping a vacuum around a tin bottle
which neither heat nor cold can reach.
Even her dress, hung over the chair,
could keep his bedroom warm for days.

Amusement

What do they know we don't? I wonder, boarding
the spaceship with Cathy's teenage daughter,
while our families, nursing their stomach aches,
sip flat cokes in the sun. Inside it's hot
as a kiln made muggy by the residue
of juveniles gone before us, respiring
en masse in the dark like wet clay heated.
Even before the room starts spinning with us
adhering to the walls, kids up in the rafters
husk their sneakers, casually snubbing
the safety rules a Fair employee speed reads
even as he kicks out the clutch. Suppose
the carney's *not* a dropout wanted for
sodomy in several southern counties,
but the vessel's alien scout who's
waited years for this particular crop
of depressed and nascently sexual:

you, arms stiff at your sides, shrinking
from the force that pins you like the weight
of your first, insensitive lover: me
upside down and yelling, while loose change
crabs up the front of my shirt and my carkeys
poke a first claw from my right front pocket.
Imagine us hurtling toward an asteroid,
fertile yet bleak as the farm goods tent
we're forced to tour with our folks, pretending

ballhead cabbage matters: where even our
flirting's some sorry inflection of despair,
mouthed and winked over lacquered gourds
and squash the girth of bombs, inedible.

Now as the floor drops away and our blood
spins out to stratified iron and water,
the vinegars of hormones and fear that drive
us fuse to a sickening concentration.
We've done too many rides, and our ages
aren't right, and your mother, who's having
second thoughts, is ready to run you home
at the first pallor of daughterly submission,
the sulk she knows one hug can cave to tears.
She knows the hardest most fugitive loves
are born in a moment of amusement.

People of Few Words

I love people of few words.
They hug with their eyes closed.
Put their heads down like runningbacks
braced for that sweet hit.

Everything's Smokey

"*What goes on is mostly character.*"
—*Ananda Coomaraswamy*

Dawn knows so surely it scares her.
Her new Rhodesian ridgeback whelp
adores her with the soft brown eyes
of our childhood mongrel: yawning,
drags the same slack belly to scratch
across the carpet. Mornings
she hears tiny, terrier toenails
clicking a happy tattoo on
the kitchen linoleum. *One candle
tipped to another is a different
wax; the flame it buds is not
a different fire.* And so her
long-boned purebred continues Smokey,
love for it, and her son's love, real
as the softening, bowed brown ribs
sunk in a muddy backyard
in Pennsylvania. The San Jose cop
who loves them both loves Smokey.
Something is nuzzling the proffered
hands of new friends. As we sleep,
the ghost of a fat little mutt
plows its nose beneath our covers.
A catbird mimicked on the porch
this morning; I swear I saw its
tail wag. And remembered mother
rapping at the porch window, beaming.

Trick

Twelve years since I knew you,
you cross a sleeping country
and slip into my dream.

The winter's last thunderstorm
pummels south Los Angeles.
All the car alarms trip off:
a passing front, a crime-burst.

Above the street, a tenant wakes.
He hears an addict trick a lock.
A trunk heels open.

I could pretend a slender space
cools above my body when I wake.
Your moist salt weight
pins me with regret.

Let expensive, triggered toys
warn us of the rain's weight.
The city will survive
one rain's small beating.

Bachelor Officers' Quarters, Dam Neck, 1987

The ocean believes I'm a good man.
When I wake from the end of world dream
it's crumbling the beach down;
climbs steadily sideways like a crab
toward my bed while alien ships
still spin up through the pines
back to the stars from where the dream comes.

Fishing boats lit up so bright
you can see men standing in a pilothouse
a mile out on the black water
steam all night just to stay in one place,
then fall back in a line, as the world turns,
as the ocean reels in its toys.

High in this house, this quiet room,
I'm waking every few hours,
blown by the boom of the ocean,
and rolling back into sleep
as into calm suicide,
pulling a green wave over me.

White Acre

(Sea of Japan, Winter 1989)

In Pusan I'll pay a Korean girl
what she asks for her hips, her limp back,
the couple of filthy words she thinks
all servicemen adore.

Underway tonight, a pilothouse
radar's warm face speaks the movements
of silent vessels, it hums beneath
my spread hands.

The color of this night has no name.
A Soviet RORSAT's white ball
glides through a phosphorescent
pepper of stars.

West of this tired world,
a different ocean of silver light
collects the constellations
when they break down,

and spills the lights of tankers,
warships, blind netted boats
back to the beaded rim
of this black sea.

Here all the moon can make
is an empty white acre of water,
where sea and slender frigate touch
as lovers should do.

Cabbage Moths Settling for the Afternoon

These small pine whites, these summer chalks
are shaking through the open louvers
of the Corners Laundromat looking for
someplace to sleep.

They tether to tablelegs, purse straps, threads,
cling, fluttering cool spots on shins.
They'll make a harbor out of anyone the wind
won't pull them off.

Nobody cares one suffers me to touch
its parched wings, it is so tired.
(We are people sitting close on the one bench
reading novels.)

No, but strum the fern of its antenna,
it will snap like firecracker dud,
stamping white thread legs. These tatters request
a close forbearance.

We humor the old woman in the housedress
to prattle of powders and change.
We share with the secreted hundreds a safe
place to fold,

to charge up for another week,
upside-down over the warm machines
that go all night spinning the world
from our worn things.

Racetrack   Downriver

Tar-heavy at twilight a smooth
Susquehanna snags herring gulls
out of the dusk; pulls their boats
downriver. A heron lays out
from the bank, ducking the moon.
Downriver in Selinsgrove,
the Friday night modified stocks
fire up with a moan like
a distant tornado, the flash
from its popping transformers
pinking the bellies of clouds.
You can imagine, over there,
a warm heaven under field lights,
the midget cars gunning past
the french fry stands, skidding through
the banked dirt curves. All our old
relatives are in from the boondocks,
Bill and Helen, Leroy and Viola,
rowdy as kids after school's done,
slapping and spilling cokes in
the stands, while the daredevils
punch through their haybales,
and buck like colts across
the infield. A cheer bursts like
fireworks over the bleachers.
No one's leaving anytime soon.
Alone, miles upriver in
the dark, we only hear the moan.

A Good Date

We walked onto the ice dams after supper,
cool floors powdered for a two-step.
Snowfall we couldn't see hissed like sparks
doused on our wet faces. Under the cliffs,
reliefers from Packerton drank and howled,
and domes of visible flakes, thick as glitter
in souvenirs from the Poconos,
flickered over cans of sterno or sticks
where fishermen hunkered in lawnchairs
over blue slots routered in the ice.
Old LV&RR railroad hands, twenty years before
the coal-heavy lighter of the roundhouse
crashed in debt by the river, each man worked
a knot of ice, each man with a bottle.
A work glove chalked and cracked offered
a fifth of Canadian's sticky pull,
while you wondered what month his oldest,
closest flannel shirt would moult, smoky
and soft as tobacco, come Spring.
We went there for privacy, would leave,
too stunned by shivering to kiss,
but the whiskered, toothless gap of grin
you left on the old guy's face when he
passed you the whiskey, and you took it,
wincing at its wax worm taste, made you
famous in my memory: that small good will
was the feeling I wanted between us,
the catch and warmth the brakeman sustained
with liquor until midnight, knowing as sweet
a line's hard tug toward the water.

Two

The ability to understand existence, the ability to try to recognize the wonder and responsibility of one's own existence, the ability to know even fractionally the most annihilating beauty, ambiguity, darkness, and horror which swarm every instant of every consciousness, the ability to accept, or the ability to defend one's self, or the ability to dare to try to assist others; all such as these, of which most human beings are cheated of their potentials, are, in most of these who even begin to discern or wish for them, the gifts or thefts of economic privilege, and are available to those of the leanest classes only by a rare and irrelevant miracle of born and surviving 'talent.'

—James Agee
Let Us Now Praise Famous Men

At the Naval Nuclear Prototype, Ballston Spa

We know you're very careful but
begins the leaflet the college
girl hands me at the stop sign,
the corner of state 67
and Fleet's Inn Road. She is cold
and a little afraid, her breath
a white pennant of body warmth
whipping in the blue before sunrise,
and it seems like the first kind words
I've received in a year, and I'd
like to set the brake and talk.
But the half dozen pickups
behind me press with the manic
insistence of a hijacker's gun,
and I peel out into a gap
in the queue, lurching toward woods
down a private road gutted
with potholes, pelting her legs
with stones. She leans toward
the next cab window grudged down
in cigarette smoke and loud radio.

They think submarines from the Hudson
drive up the creek at night to fuel
in secret under the geodesic dome,
and that is what the red light
means, pulsing above the forest
miles from town. From a hill you
can see the black pressure hulls beached
a hundred-and-fifty miles from sea,

the thick dew boiling from their backs.
Nautilus prototype D1G,
heavy and cold in its modernist
tun of brominated water
and stainless steel, idles
in the southern Adirondacks:
scrammed, spent, inert.

We pass the newsletter at muster
and snicker, and look for some
description of pale young men who drive
the back roads in shifts after dark,
or mine the cold cases for links
and beer in the Acme alone
late Saturday nights—who rent by
the month then suddenly move: how
one was reported at sunrise
at the end of a set of straight
tire tracks punched in a field,
seat heeled back, the windows rolled
down, listening to the sleet.

Temporary Duty for Instruction,
our fourth move in as many years,
we progress toward a Fleet
growing ever more distant and
suspect, moving by increments
further into the country.

Shaking from the last failed drills
on our twelve-hour shift's one break
in a corner of the compound,
I can still feel the hate in my
LPO's grip at the console,

fingers still blanched in arrest
on my wrist, when the first of
the protesters, running downhill
through the woods, stops just short
of the electric fence, grins
and throws wheat in our faces—

staggering back in remorse
like high school toughs in the malls,
baiting then backing from a fight.
Like people on skates sailing
backward: that look on our
faces as lungsful of smoke
ladle from throats in disappointment,
and the young women stare at our
prisonblue dungarees, our shined
cracked boondockers curled
at the steel toes. *We know you're*
very careful, but everyone
makes mistakes, the argument goes.

One word out of anyone, and one
of these hardlooking squids will break
down, croak out the last ten years
of his life in an epic
of recession and betrayal:
the interviews crashing badly
in silence, courses withdrawn from,
father's wills: the handshake and perfect
empathy, recruiters' smooth lies.

As the DOD police step in
with dogs and shouldered M-16's,
and the chant picks up as scripted,

we're ordered back into the plant
with folded lunchbags, leaflets, butts
policed from the ground, checking,
as repetition trains, for
the little luminescent detectors
clipped to our belts, which tell
us each month just how little
this line of work affects us.

And as the upstate wilds of New York
state break into ferocious color,
I climb up the ladder and seal
myself under a pressure hatch,
crawl deep into monitored twists
of main and aux and gland steam,
rigging for reduced electrical
load as the next round of drills
commences, with my full deal
of technical books and mission
to memorize it all by December:
silent and conserving effort,
like a deep boat rigged for ultra-
quiet in Rickover's vision
of a warship steaming under
almost perpetual propulsion.

Deep Depth

You learned, when Father yelled,
how to step out of your body.
He cursed your life, you entered
a space inside the walls.
Mummy boy, you could see
each room of the house from there,
carpet and clock, and even
your own self, strangely waxen,
shirtsleeves hanging like the empty
arms of a coat on a painted pole.
For years they couldn't find you.

You lived with blind mice
and ghosts of dutch aunts
speaking homespun and lethal
wisdom: *Father knows best.*
Mother stands for comfort.
May the crimes of our children
be visited upon them
by their own kids, sevenfold.

A hand falls like a moon
close to your face, waking you.
You are in a submarine.
You are the emergency.
The officers are shouting,
trying to pull you in,
crushed but alive, out of all
that tremendous pressure.

Submariners

1

Months at a time we have all gone down
to a secret place beyond the Outer Banks,
and practiced the grisly deaths of our friends.
Shock and radiation and steam deaths,
and the gray muscle falling from the bone.
We let our own thoughts die down in fatigue,
we rinse our dungarees under steam drains,
the stale smell of the superheat
tapped off the high pressure header
like the sear, sour, and desiccated
atmosphere of our planets
that makes me think there's nothing after death.
In the center of the ship the reactor
goes on seething and demanding,
fission like a process of the mind
smoldering in massless consumption,
rod bank a bridle steam a yoke
pulling the ship across the violet fields.
Night is a phenomenon of surface,
and the days keep shedding hours.

2

Forward the men share bunks one sleeps one
dreams of the night of cool berthing,
where light is never seen for months,
that gives the illusion of a windswept woods
in which Petty Officer Cassada makes me
a pallet, his warm sheets broken to a softness,

like dry leaves trampled and moldering,
or the talc of straw in a dog's coop.
A picture of pale, drawn daughters
is clasped between oil thumbprints
in the margins of the Corinthians,
his white Bible hung on a lanyard.
My first night down in the *Rickover,*
I found the glossy journals on the pillow.
One was Italian and showed "*Pissing!*"
bodies wet and cringing. On wet grass
a woman lay down with a collie,
free hand holding its head down.
The machinist mate looked at me hurt.
"What's the matter, pal, you don't read smut?"
and couldn't I take a gift.
He'd worked forty hours and couldn't sleep,
just sat listening for things to break.
The boat tipped forward in the dark,
a corkscrew digging for pressure.

3

During the months of this slowest flight,
the port turns banking for days,
I fantasize desperate tender acts
and talk to men blasted with stress
in the warm and sour darkness,
men breathing on shelves all around us.
Some count the days of their indenture
on small chains coiled in their pockets.
Some lend me tools and clean skivvies.
They know I've a solemn commission

working down the ranks and offices
to conn the easy frigates,
and won't be here much longer.
They linger now after the failed drills,
young first class petty officers,
conspiring their final enlistments,
and looking up to me for confirmation,
their faces in the bottom bunks' light
whispering watchful and furtive
like faces above a lantern in a grave.

Running   Ultra   Quiet

Underway from Toulon,
I sat outboard the turbines on midwatch,
the whole crew asleep,
the boat like a man dreaming,
under black tons.

The engine room brilliant—
live steam in the header made a sound
like a shower of snow.
I cradled my head on the lagging
and shivered with heat.

I know what submariners
daydream at sea. Not the lover in the bed,
but the safety of the room.
In ours the blinds bumped on the windowsills,
patting the wind down.

Off the French coast that morning
water on deck in shaft alley tasted salt.
I swung into my rack
and lay awake while the boat climbed
seawater hills,

unable to forget,
and thumbed an Italian fuck mag.
I had nothing else,
and was beginning in my curtained bunk
to feel safe as the dead.

Warships

Long Beach refinery's twin fires
snuff and reflame, seem to smother
in this morning's high, thin fog.
Steeped in fume, cars boil on Highway 1,
lurch and grind to Torrance and back.
In the liquor store, don't say good morning
to Chicanos, they can't talk to you.
The blacks they don't owe you.
And the smirk on your white neighbor's face
lets you know how well he's coped.
Everyone sing, the sun is everything golden.

Only on the piers, amphibious ships
lay in nest like horses standing together
in a cold barn, bellies touching.
They are serene, they welcome war.

Deploy becomes a word like *Liberty*,
the thought of a drink that pulls you through a day.
Evenings the violent sounds pour in,
screeching tires outside the Topless Club,
the divorced man stabbing at her doorbell,
a power saw crying on a piece of wood
that won't give, and is always fed with more.

Night in the Box

Returning to port too late
to arrange for a pilot or tug,
our Captain would pencil a box
on the SoCal chart, a few
hundred acres of water
our two night bridge teams
might let the ship graze in
while he slept. Nowhere were watches
longer than that dark range
tucked behind leeward Catalina,
all shipping tracking east
in lanes and Avalon's hourly
ferries roped in Wilmington
docks for the night. You
could feel a tired resistance
in the obstacles of khaki and must
slouched in the blackened pilothouse
as we rigged for dark and screwed
the rubber boot down
over the surface search radar,
the officers of deck and conn
resigning themselves to the bridgewings,
turning every half hour to spool
a softly unraveling wake.

Unthinkable, not to turn,
to push into the great black
like a satellite seething
through empty space, the ocean
for four hundred miles
snared with traffic schemes

and undersea cables,
gunnery ranges and anchorages,
whole estates of prohibited
Navy zones like paved
and sewered future suburbs
in a desert below Los Angeles.
I longed for cold Aleutians
as my teenage lookouts—
drugged with an hour of sleep
and sick for shore—dropped
the outbound beads of late
departures, the Mobil
George   Washington   Bridge,
in the monied high shimmer
of Palos Verdes. Sometimes
I ordered rudder without
course, just spun.

And just as the ensign and I
with practice could almost feel
in the altered rhythm of pitch
our frigate cross our CO's
line, or could have believed
a border lay like oil
across the water, so some
men must have felt in the bow's
panoramic swing across
the shipyard cranes, refinery
flames, and amber murk
of Long Beach one more
inport workweek check
the natural drift of their lives.

Fifty miles out
I'd seen the stack lights
pulse in a fibril of gas:
the continent's golden seam
would open to let us
back in, someday.

(to the crew of the USS Lewis B. Puller,
1987–1991)

Sea Smoke

A hundred miles west of Washington,
the moon coasts at twenty-twenty knots
above the broken forest of the fog.

Surfaces, and the fog tows it under,
the white aluminum back of a salmon
striking upstream through white water.

Inside the dark pilothouse, the Coast Guard
channel chatters of a prairie of clear sea
from Point St. George to Cape Flattery.

It is twelve-thirty in the morning.
My lookout, Drew, is asleep, an oval of low
warmth spreading from his cheek against the window.

We wake him, and send him topside.
The moon breaks free into a deep black bay.
A tanker's green light low in the sky

must be the window of a house on a plain:
I think I see Drew dropping down from the forecastle,
the thin voice of the boatswain mate

scratching in the phones left coiled on deck
as Drew walks home. Startled,
a milk white hare skips over the waves.

Drunks Handling Lines in Seattle

We're so low in the order of battle,
when the squadron hits town for Fleet Week
they berth us down by the sulfur piles,
pier in the hundred-and-somethings,

canary yellow hills of ore and Rainier's
cap in the distance a pale pink spaceship
hovering in smog. Underway already Sunday
morning, the local reservists don't show,

so we shout awake the little piles of clothes
slumped against the sunny sides of quonsets.
The drunks scrape up to the bits, budge
the mooring lines over the bollards

with a heave like a simple letting-fall,
a motion that seems strangely practiced.
They seem sobered to be suddenly so needed.
They look dutiful as seamen, and as inward.

Men in whites manning the radar decks,
blue missile on the rail, there's only
these homeless men to see us off.
How silly and yet somehow familiar

we must look, sliding too slowly from the pier,
four hundred foot guided missile frigate
irrelevant in all our late weapons,
like a building full of outrageous toys,

or the clean, early promise of a life
too expensive and disciplined for you
to have lived, the thought of which
you must give up again every so often;

a sleek ship of clean-shaven men,
which every now and then needs a favor,
embarrassed young ensign on the flight deck
waving thank you, sirs, for letting us go.

Return to Port, December

A school of brown and silver mackerel
rakes the deep clear water off the Mole
along the two miles I walk from my ship
to my car dozing under three months' dust.

I'm talking to my mother with my hands
and a voice in my head tinier
than the thin current beating in an earphone
of a radio whispering to no one,

saying how much I love—no, relish—
our lives today. Seventeen states away
my mother has left her bathwater and sits,
in damp nightgown, in front of the television.

Maybe it's freezing in the yard outside,
and a house draft rubs its cool muzzle against
her temple, waking her, for a moment,
from a long dull dream of sixty years.

Now she knows my happiness; thinks All
the wasted time, like a school of fish, changes,
suddenly and in sync, its course:
slim and shining minutes reversing the years.

Preacher's Camp

A hundred feet up the fire road,
I can still hear the knock of a bass boat
drifting on the lake. Minutes later,
sunlight in rhythm stripes oaks

a half mile deep into the woods
as a wake rocks ashore, thumping and leaching
topsoil clenched in the roots of yellow birch.
The camp is under the reservoir; a road

planes out of the water. A hurt runs on
in the mind in made up conversations:
the structures submerged and unseen,
the shores we walked down to.

Something no longer there continues in something
hidden: lake light swings through the dark beneath pines.
The shock of a deer's hooves striking rock
runs straight through the ground and rattles a heart.

Packerton

Pain is not the river sliding black and gold
below Packerton mountain's dark back.
Pain lingers in blue snow backwaters,
the deeper, permanent cold of ground
stinging back the open hands of ice.
The township's last black bear, oiled fur
drilled by parasites, crouches in terror
of daylight in an ash can under the Conrail
trestle. White rails ring hunger and rabies
prowls the Long Run dump in packs of stray
white dogs. Dump trucks rumble down sandy
state roads, too heavy to brake for deer.
Their partial carcasses, frozen,
remind us of doomed stone ovens
Iroquois abandoned. It is a pain
of slate blue hills, their forests of stone.

Snow won't stick to white metal backs
of our houses. They withstand each evening's
slap of cold, like the faces of teenage
daughters, indifferent, eyes open. I nail
a strand of colored lights in coils
of barbed wire around my parents' doors.
Their faded faces stare from within,
convinced I'm good inside. Moored in salted
driveways, Chryslers' lacquered hoods endure,
polished and brittle as each father's
sense of his own guilt. I stand in my
parents' front yard, hammer in hand.

Backyard beagles curled into springs of bone
die in their coops another night. In their dreams,
tremendous snapping turtles crawl, driven
by hunger, up the thawed banks from the river.
Christmas lights stop blinking, buoyed in wind.
Tonight the deer, who live a thousand years,
come down from their country to watch us.
In fields behind factory parking lots
they turn to stone, their eyes wicked opals.
Only the river still moves, bright through black
land bared to a golden sky: cold and slow
as our gestures toward any neighbor,
golden and wide as the feeling we're
sure we've offered, sure we deserve.

Incident

Off the dirt road off Mansion House Hill Road,
a Packerton town cop's blue light strobes
a space like a warehouse culled in the fir
by twenty years of lovers necking along
the dam. The ceiling the pine branches make
is the height of a hippie van and rainproof,
and a dry rug of needles pressed by cars
keeps snow out and holds a kind of warmth.
The cop works the late shift, alone, rousing
the transients, asking the teenagers' names,
utility light like a firehose
busting the couples apart. No one answers
his knock on the windshield of the jacked-up
Dodge Charger, cold beneath an even glaze
of sleet, and so he plies a scraper
from the borough car, noticing between
blue licks of its beacon a garden hose
duct-taped to the tailpipe, looping
to the right rear fender.
                                         He's seen
the grisly thing, bums who've drunk themselves
to jelly, frozen flat to the seat;
sometimes not bums, the Pennsylvania highways
stunned with factories boarded and locked.
Hardship is no one's stranger, they say here,
and Donnelly, chipping at 5 a.m.
through ice a lifetime deep can't see
the jug of Riunite on the gearbox,
the bag of grass, or the blue ceramic

embrace of naked bodies, his daughter
and the hophead from Weissport, but figures
the gas tank's empty, frost takes time to build,
and some poor bastard did one thing right.

The Chrysler

Our parents were always fighting,
in a Chrysler like a steel cell,
the summer we saw every state.

It got to a point, just by saying
our names our father brought bruises.
His sigh left a hidden red burn.

Mother's hands tearing her dry hair
out of absolute frustration
were young hands in pouches of seed

that labored throughout that August
to plant pain across a continent.
Fifteen years later, we can hear

madmen still shouting from bathtubs
in Route One Florida motels,
madwomen weeping in shame

in small Pennsylvania towns
where all the hell's night long
kitchen lights are burning. Sisters,

if there was life on Mars I'd hock
everything I owned to take that rocket.
But all we have is California,

where the winter rain which whitens
the streets is too simple, too rare
to sustain the larger voices.

Rondeau

She goes to bed after supper,
avoiding the fight with Marvin.
When I wake up it'll be better
she says. She's been
saying it for forty years.

Sits in her slip draws the insulin,
straps the arm works the syringe in,
a modest kind of dying when
she goes to bed.

And drifting beneath the comforter
in the one kind place God made for her,
imagines grim northern in-laws frozen
in theirs. She'll order the children:
When I go, don't put me on no cold mountain!
She'll notice both shock and smirk before
she goes to bed.

New Pain on the River

Sometimes the hook sets too far down,
the mouth is too small to work
a finger in, I've forgotten
the needlenose pliers in the car.

The fish, always an immature
rainbow, small olive river chub
or fallfish, gets perfectly still
in my hand, a trust which always

makes it shake some, trying to force
down the hook to unsnag the barb.
There's the sound of little leather tearing,
a hiccup; after, a little clear blood.

The creek runs loud with last night's rain;
a heron glides across; the leaves
of cottonwoods clatter and flash.
The hook always comes out somehow.

Loosely in my hand still in the stream
now, the small thing won't swim away;
it seems to hesitate; its whole world
is different now, less certain.

Expecting its whip-away, I let
the water grab it, but it lists,
scuttling, and flashing white belly,
the current twirling it quickly

downstream even as I hiss
a fast prayer. (*Compassion for all
things,* said the Enlightened One;
though our God said no such thing.)

Coming out before a workday
to love the land, and put down,
for a little time, worry, thus
I inject new pain into the river.

Lehighton

the Jaycee Peewee League:
Army, Navy, Air Force, and
Notre Dame

Tonight in the valley
stadium lights forge
a bracelet of bright stones.

Talking too fast to breathe,
their mouths wanting air,
little mock cheerleaders

run home along the highway
holding their sides. Headlights
gather them out of dark,

lift the small bodies, turn
and gently set them down,
like a dream of fondling

in the fey and delicate
mind of a twelve year old.
The Knee-Hi football boys,

the sleek backs, the chubby
guards and linebackers all
must be limping through town

on clotted cleats now up
Mahoning Street's long haul.
Everyone laughing, dead tired.

It's after ten, Navy
beat Notre Dame again,
the crowd smells gas and turf:

and out by the silent
highway, the green and gold
of the little cheerleaders

mimics a team they know
is for real and is not theirs.
Something makes them stare

with the calm, disappointed
faces of mill women
into headlights that shortly

blind them. Everyone
has grown old suddenly.
Now all the pretty things

white wool sweaters pleats
friends are only borrowed,
and must be shown good care.

Coop

The boy comes home to find the chain
limp on its stake. He picks up one end
and pulls, unzipping the link from the frozen
dirt. Then he takes a stone and breaks the ice
surface of the dog's dish, pours the water
and uneaten food's soft larvae on the ground.
Inside the coop, nut-like sacks of spider's
eggs cluster in the slack corner webs.
The straw has been trampled to powder,
and in it the boy finds prehistoric bones,
mildewed knuckles, licked to a polish.
The bones retain a varnish of spit,
and the straw feels warm though the cold outside
pricks the boy's ankles, and his kneecaps sting.
He thinks: a dog's life begins new each day,
starts in hunger, ends shivering into sleep,
the black night starless and the sleep
broken by distant sounds. Morning comes, dog
wakes, hungry. One day the boy's father
unhooks the heavy chain from its collar
and leads it to the car where it musn't go,
whispering encouragement. The boy cleans out
the coop that night, discovering among
the things the dog carried there, an argyle
sock from his newest and favorite pair.

Child Witness

Who put felony in eight-year-old fingers,
short-nailed and hard as fork tines drumming
the table in the teachers' lounge her mother
and I have commandeered, ordering
a puzzled reading teacher to wait? Back
of the school, the sun is still as dark
as scarlet crayon you can look at,
seeping through black Crozet hickories
half a mile from the Amway plant. Inside,
all the colored chairs are shouldered to their tables,
everything bright and aching for more sleep.
She ain't talking so I'll have to. Not a cop,
not from her school, not even a real lawyer yet,
I'm trying to get a judge to make some rules,
get her mom's clothes from the house, her ballglove
and maybe the Barbie Jeep. I tell her
I'm someone my own mother never had,
needed and didn't know how to find; and as her
head slides to her arms I'm ashamed my voice
starts trembling, miss too much the kind and careful
fingers caressing her fists, that touch
that cures all anger and self-loathing.
In a minute she'll buck up, trot us out
into the battered van, our dress shoes slipping
in spilled popcorn, and tell us who was last
behind the wheel, how far they rolled downhill
when daddy bolted to chase mom, how she
slipped her belt to grab the brake, her sisters
screaming in their car seats, before they hit—

looking back at mom to check she got the story
right, though her voice is still as timid
as a night station probing for reception,
steeped in a static of brutally competitive
broadcasts. What can I say she'll understand
to show her the gravity of my respect; how
pledge this family the hunger of my jealousy?
Can't call her little princess, princesses
wear skirts, have highlights kissed in their hair,
don't eat off of washed paper plates in a two
room emergency rental on the highway.
And that other word is *his* word, is colored
construction-paper sunflowers taped
to the classroom wall because you have to,
forgotten in a week, curling in clutter
and moot reminders pressed to refrigerator
doors. All the best ones are taken,
so I promise her to get them money.

A Reading

Just when the worst is recorded and stilled,
you remember the *Why?* of a screendoor
reeling open, teased hair snagged
in a mad mother's fist: your toughest
youngest sister, late from school again.
You listen to a woman read a story
to twenty silent people at a college,
and think of sisters whispering behind locked doors
weeknights a grim man climbs the front steps,
workclothes in a shopping bag. Everyone
has braced for the fight, the father barking *Slut!*
and nobody moves, but inside something gives,
releasing its soundless riot of hurt
like a capsule breaking softly in the stomach.
And you know some words like a war's lost
bombs, corroding submerged in pasture, will
go off every so many years. Like when that
sister, whom you love, who writes of every
caring and capable man she'll break up with
two weeks after each time you visit
in letters you should probably throw away,
calls from California after midnight.
Now you're thirty, she's thirty-five,
and you listen to her usual soft petition
against the years and slights ticking
above the drizzle through an open window,
the sound of water failing again
to rise above the earth. Though tonight
it's a voice hailing straight from the woods

of a girl who missed the bus and panicked,
and ran home cutting through a cemetery,
as she tells someone, for the first time,
what three boys made her do behind a stone.

Bless These

Years later Fern Meifarth still bangs out
the first chord wrong: we lurch into a carol
like people in a bus hit from behind.

A hard note rockets like a loose balloon:
the children's chorus—two sisters and a shy friend—
look at their shoes again singing softly.

At odd times our pastor waves baby hands,
stirring something up, or patting it down,
I don't know which. Nothing has changed:

six, or twenty-seven, in a back pew, giggling,
while an elf girl tries to catch with her tongue
the wax bouncing off my candle nub's cardboard hilt.

Alone among front pews this year, old, kind women
are pruned of sole children and husbands
whose names have joined the names of the old Dutch

remembered in a banner of altar poinsettias
or the whispered request for a convalescent prayer.
Shall We Gather at the River, I'd request,

to speak, in prayer. No, we sing *Silent Night*.
This night is quiet, sure. Behind red glass,
heavy wind brings colder weather,

a few doe rummage in the blown down fields,
the old roads lap this block with veins of marble,
and black, swept porches await their single lights.

Debt

No one ever mentioned
the cost of so much
solitude and distance.

The daily *No* of office staffs,
families' matriarchal packs,
homeowners territorial.

And the months the only words spoken
are with salesmen,
cashiers, telemarketers.
Every human contact
a tiny accrual of debt.

Staff Sergeant Woodrow Staudt

Some asshole at Monte Casino,
a kid, a pisspants, mid-charge
and blind out of love for America,
shot him in the back.

Before, it was Libya, naked
behind a German cattle fence,
pelvis dwindling like milk in a bowl,
shorn skull burnt madder.

When he and the other guy busted out
it was night and they ran among spiders,
kicking then cutting the boots off the green
bloated dead.

Squatting under a horseblanket eating
dry cornflakes, forty years ago.
How could this be a life's logo,
anchor, a bottle

of grimness pulled on again and again?
The local women laughed, said
Woody got his pecker shot off
and it made him shy.

Pinto Way, Orlando, at least
there's sand. Now that he's dying alone,
what else can he think about, hearing
the sand fleas hopping?

Franklin   Heights

Someone must know the top of this hill,
to find the marker this far from the road.
He's brushed the new snow off, left a pine wreath.
Township zoning law forbids upright stones
to keep our dead uniform, like parked cars,
though many could afford just a railroad spike.
Winters this hill is bald to the weather,
a snowfield where plastic poinsettias
and black World War stars grow out bent from wind.

Between the red school for the retarded,
now boarded shut, and the weedy slope down
to Motola's bar, I walk around lost,
and can't find a single broke uncle's grave,
or the grandmother pinned by the frozen
weight of her breasts, her great Dutch bosom
known to smother squirming children.
I've swept off too many bronze plates
that begin with name and year but don't end.

Hillsides turn blue as temperatures dive,
shadowing Lenape Indian graves
the human mind has lost. Someday developers
will buy this land cheap and pave it under.
Someone will move, the silk flowers mildew.
Still, someone's footprints etch a crumbling line
in snow to her parents. Like a cold kiss,
one real red poinsettia flames while it dies.

Waterfall

Ithaca, NY

Radiance has come to my mother's face.
Up from Pennsylvania for a day trip,
she hasn't stopped praising the waterfalls,
thrilled by the slow white river
spreading in skeins down the black shale
face of mountain off the highway; thrilled
by the park's gutted grist mill, millshaft
broken in its pinions; the trees whose names
I teach her; the question of baldy cypress
I ask that cradles her south to a blacksnake
swamp two barefoot girls ran heedless,
the thought of which, just for a moment,
stills the little tune of her shivering.
We have driven to the top of this mountain
in a boatlength Chrysler Newport, a blue
rose tablecloth covering the good front seat.
I have buttoned my mother's coat at the collar
because her hands won't do right in this cold,
and walked her across the park's brittle lawn
toward *the really steep* falls I have promised her.
Today, she must keep both eyes on her feet,
for they balk like two bad pets in tow,
one pulling, the other refusing to come,
interrupting her story of her best
friend Jean, lost in the muffled, sudden sleet
of an old world war's first shrapnel.

"I've gone this far, I'm not going back!" she says.

Two hundred yards down a path around a bend
where I have gone ahead to count the steps,

my father has come to tell me what facts
I've avoided: it isn't asthma teased by cold,
but a heart the both of us imagine
grinding slowly down in disrepair
in that uneasy place where he and I
have learned to conserve old feuds, alone.
How many months will I relive the walk back
by the muddy, half-frozen creek to the place
where this tiny woman turns, alone and pleased?
She grins up into the frozen burst
of a single yellow poplar, whose
lovelier name, *tulip tree,* I have—
reversing the protocol of age and teaching
names—taught her. A hundred yards behind,
creek, woods, shale inexplicably let go
in a sudden resignation to gravity,
freefalling in beauty, just beyond our range.

After Tragedy

The Earth collected its lonely.
The wind pulled tight its cord of sand
and buried the beach's sleeping drunks.
We dared not go near the water.

Placid as fawns the paired people witnessed
a running man stall for breath,
his collarbones broken by heat. They watched
another man sink through the street—

and my own face turned like a scuttled boat
still above the sidewalk whispering
kind words, love poems, threats,
the paisley that floated on my last breath.

Mounting our empty beds at night we heard
the dirt already raining on the rooftop.

Fibrillation

The hours say no more homebody, Ruth.
Your poor plan breaks down. No more hunched
in night gown, tea before the milk light
of the television, nursing this breath.

Medevacs ferry in the infinite accidents
outside your ACU. You hear them fall toward
your roof, captured by misery's gravity.
When you can talk, you count us like chicks.

You are teaching us the mother's-heart sutra:
No old age and death, no end to old age and death.
No food for three weeks, pancreatis from
the catheter, stomach a bubble of pain.

No speech, your mouth fills with sand.
No beauty, twenty pricks a day, puppet
hands in harness dad will put white gloves
upon, blisters clouding the collapsed veins.

No turning, no bending that leg, the tube
holding open the artery must be straight.
No cause for or end to suffering, no natural
day and night, three weeks at Lehigh Valley,

then: no operation.
Swimmer, drowning in your heart, you tread
interminable nights alone, while we scour
wrong parts of the ocean, pointing our weak lights.

We begin to live harder the better
to bring you some fresh offer from the living,
whisper how we've fed the wild geese at home
from our hands, those durable engines

of continental flight, precarious on land,
their bellies wagging over splayed feet,
their skinny tongues rasping our palms,
besting their fear, trusting us, that hungry.

Late tonight, your heart will batter itself
to pieces trying to fly out with them.

Milt

*He was such a bastard toward everyone
later on. You were the only one
he let sit on his lap.*

—Barbara

The hex on the black barn
says *Ruh*—
its painted quails
stars and Dutch flowers
scrubbed to the boards
by endless rain.

Red leaves and rain
are hitting the Studebaker,
water spreads like a wing
of silver tears
across the car windows.

The hills are undivided.
The small house is dark.
Milt's face shines
like a trail of pearl
some sad, exotic
wood snail has laid
upon the barn walls.
The soft rain breaks
and lengthens the pearl,
and washes the black boards,
you are losing,
Milt, the weather
has worked its change too long
for my spread hands
to shelter you.

Rescue

Finally, she clung to the bed rail
as if it were the side of a lifeboat,
weary from treading her bedclothes,
and the tow of arterial catheter,
insulin and prednisone drip. Doctors,
those stern boatswains, shook their heads.
Summer already lay too heavy
with longsuffering, and needed
to lighten its load of care, and float
a sparer party home. For twenty
more nights we would watch the procession
of sine waves roll across her monitor,
those ardent crests ticking harder,
crumbling and deforming in the darkness,
as an ocean of silent disappointments
threw its last waves down in protest.

Allentown,   Pennsylvania
August 11, 1997

About the poet

David Staudt grew up in a Pennsylvania German
family in rural northeastern Pennsylvania. He has
spent eight years in the Navy as an enlisted
submariner and as an officer on a frigate in the Pacific.
He graduated from Princeton and later studied at
Cornell, where he received an MFA in writing, and
won the Corson-Bishop Poetry Prize as well as an
Academy of American Poets Award. He taught writing
at Cornell and at Susquehanna University as a Lecturer
before earning a law degree at the University of
Virginia in 1999.

For the last twenty years his poems, stories, and essays
have appeared in literary magazines, and he has been
nominated five times for the Pushcart Prize.

The Gifts and Thefts is his first book-length
publication.